# Diet recommendations for Nutrition of the infant - supplementary food

Please check these recommendations always with a nutrition consultant, therapist, doctor or dietician. The recipes and the list of ingredients are supporting the conventional medical therapy.
The calorie disclosures of fresh ingredients (fruit and vegetables) vary according to quality and time of harvest. The contents were checked by a dietician and a nutrition consultant for the Traditional Chinese Medicine (TCM).

Author:
©2017 Josef Miligui
www.ebns.at

Source:
The lists are created from the EBNS database for nutritional counseling. The database is used by dietitians, therapists and doctors for advising the patient / client.

Literature:
The specialist literature and the training documents of the German and Austrian dietary and traditional Chinese medicine serve as a knowledge base. We have used the documents as a basis of knowledge, adapted it to our experience and completed them.
http://di-book.com

Title Photo:
©2008 Erika Weixlbaumer

Production and publishing:
BoD – Books on Demand, Norderstedt
ISBN: 9783752811193

# Diet recommendations for DIETETICS - Universal - Nutrition of the infant - supplementary food

# 1   Treatment strategy

Baby food (other than breast milk and infant milk)
In the first 4 to 6 months of life, exclusive milk nutrition (mother milk, industrial infant milk) is recommended.
Supplementary food before the fifth month of life increases the risk of developing an allergy.
From about 6th month: early carrot, pumpkin, zucchini
From about 7th month: pear, apple, banana, beef or poultry meat
From about 8.month: broccoli, fennel, cucumber, lamb, corn, spelled, oat, millet
From about 9.month: cauliflower, spinach, water or honey melon
From ca.10.Month: Kohlrabi, apricot - As a fat supplement, rapeseed oil is recommended.

A dairy meal is replaced month by month by a porridge meal.
Month-by-month, a milk meal is replaced by a meat meal: vegetable potato meat porridge, a milk-cereal mash and a cereal-fruit mash.
According to the German Society for Nutrition, the caloric requirement of a toddler is about 1100 kcal per day.
Something more accurate you could also calculate it:
for boys 104 kcal, for girls 108 kcal per kg body weight per day.

# 2   Avoid

Chicken egg, cow's milk, fish, citrus fruits, nuts, wheat, celery, chocolate.
Use only low fat and salt.
Onions, cabbage, fried and legumes should not be given until the second year of life.

# 3   Breakfast

kkal. per serving
Apple sauce with raisins - from 6th month ....................................... 73
Carrot juice - from the 12th week...................................................... 69
Carrots with potato foam - from 8 months...................................... 316
Cherry cereal porridge - from the 8th month ................................. 219
Fruit jelly - from the 8th month......................................................... 60
Grape compote - from the 8th month.............................................. 128
Grape juice (fresh, homemade)........................................................ 73
Milk mash for the bottle - from the 8th month................................ 187
Milk-free cereal fruit porridge - from the 8th month........................ 220
Month porridge - from 7th month .................................................... 157

# 4   Snack

# 5   Lunch

# 6   Afternoon

# 7   Dinner

# 8   Any time

# 9  Recipes

(recommendable) = You can use more.
(little) = You should use less than specified or omit.

## 9.1  Apple sauce with raisins - from 6th month

Stops diarrhea, promotes digestion, appetizing, relieves diarrhea,
activates carbohydrate metabolism.
Cooking time approx. 25 min
Calories p. portion: 74
10 portions
Allergens: O

**Quantity of ingredients**
Apple (sweet)  2,2 lbs /  1000g. (recommended)
Water  1/2 cup /  100g. (yes)
Raisins  1/8 lbs - 2oz /  50g. ()

**Cooking instructions:**
Wash, peel and quarter the apples and remove the core. Put the apples
with the water in a pot. Wash the raisins with hot water and add them.
Cook at low heat for about 10 minutes, then allow to cool. For children
up to 10 months, mash in the blender finely. For the larger ones, crush
with the potato steamer. Fill and seal in a freezer or empty yoghurt jug.
Close the yoghurt jug. Freeze in the shock freezer.
If necessary, thaw at room temperature for about 6 hours. (Lasting
about 4 months).
The fruit mousse is intended as dessert or intermediate meal. It has an
anti-digestive effect. In case of diarrhea give better banana.

## 9.2  Baby milk - up to 6 months

Little laxative, strengthens kidney and bladder, diuretic, warming the
body from the inside, expands blood vessels, strengthens the muscles,
regulates internal organs functions. Nourishes and strengthens body.
Cooking time approx. 10 min
Calories p. portion: 118
1 portions
Allergens: G

**Quantity of ingredients**
Water  1/2 cup /  100g. (yes)
Rice mash  1 table spoon /  5g. (yes)

Cow's milk (whole milk 3.5% fat)  1/2 cup /  100g. ()
Pear juice  1/2 oz /  15g. ()
Corn germ oil  1 teaspoons /  3g. (little)

**Cooking instructions:**
Put the water in a small saucepan. Stir in the rice pudding and place the
pot on the cooking surface. Heat till it boils over medium heat and
simmer for 2-3 minutes. Remove the pot from the heat, beat the milk
with a whisk, add the pear juice and mix everything. Add the oil and
beat the milk vigorously with the electric hand mixer. (For baby
lukewarm cool and put in a vial).

## 9.3   Banana porridge - from the 18th month (in summer)

Regulates gastrointestinal function. Protects the digestive system.
Detoxifying, affects anorexia, good to fight flatulence, inflammatory
bowel disease.
Cooking time approx. 10 Min
Calories p. portion: 235
1 portions
Allergens: AG

**Quantity of ingredients**
Water  1/2 cup /  125g. (yes)
Wheat flakes  1/2 oz /  20g. (yes)
Banana  1/4 lbs - 4oz /  100g. (recommended)
Butter organic  1 table spoon /  10g. (little)

**Cooking instructions:**
Mix the water with the flakes in a small pan. Bring to boil by low heat,
cook for 1-2 minutes and then remove from the cooking area. Cut the
banana in pieces into the pot, add the butter and puree with a blender.
Fill the banana porridge into a plate (feed the baby with the spoon).
(The afternoon porridge is basically cooked only with water, so it is all
the more important not to forget to add fat, otherwise your baby is
hungry long before the next meal.)
Instead of butter, you can also take corn oil - especially when the
porridge is not so hot, the oil is distributed more easily.
If you use buckwheat, millet, corn or rice flakes instead of wheat flakes,
the mash is gluten-free.

## 9.4   Carrot juice - from the 12th week

Promotes digestion, promotes spleen and liver, strengthens immune system, good for cholesterol diet.
Cooking time approx. 20 min
Calories p. portion: 69
3 portions
Allergens:

**Quantity of ingredients**
Carrot (Early Carrot)  1,3 lbs /  400g. (recommended)
Water  2 table spoons /  0g. (yes)
Orange  2 pieces /  200g. ()
Corn germ oil  1/2 teaspoon /  2g. (little)

**Cooking instructions:**
Clean the fresh carrots, wash thoroughly and peel. Steam in 3 tablespoons of water for about 15 minutes and juice in a juicer (centrifuge).
From the 1st year: Mix this carrot juice in equal parts with freshly squeezed orange juice, so that your child gets enough vitamin C otherwise with water. Whisk the juice with 1/2 teaspoon corn oil, freeze portions in an ice cube scoop. Frozen, the juice is stable for up to 6 weeks.

## 9.5   Carrots with potato foam - from 8 months

Promotes spleen and liver, reduces blood pressure, strengthens immune system. Improves digestion, regenerates skin, supports urination, lowers cholesterol, promotes the production of stool and urine, strengthens blood, strengthens nerves.
Cooking time approx. 30 min
Calories p. portion: 316
1 portions
Allergens: G

**Quantity of ingredients**
Carrot (Early Carrot)  3/8 lbs - 6oz /  150g. (recommended)
Pork meat  1/8 lbs - 2oz /  40g. (yes)
Potato (mealy)  1/4 lbs - 4oz /  100g. (recommended)
Butter organic  1 table spoon /  10g. (little)
Honey  1/2 teaspoon /  2g. (little)
Anise (Common Fennel)  1 pinch /  0,2g. (recommended)
Water  2 table spoons /  20g. (yes)

**Cooking instructions:**
Clean the carrots, wash thoroughly, peel thinly and cut into thin slices.
Cut the meat into strips.
Wash the potatoes, cook in a small saucepan with little water in about
15 minutes.
Melt half of the butter in a saucepan, fry the carrots and the meat in it. If
necessary, add 2-3 tablespoons of water, put the lid on and cook
everything over low heat in about 15 minutes.
Add the honey, the anise and the remaining butter and remove the pot
from the heat.
Peel the potatoes and press directly onto the plate with the potato
press. Distribute the honey carrots over it.


## 9.6   Cherry cereal porridge - from the 8th month

Regulates gastrointestinal function, improves blood circulation, reduces
Inflammation, moisturizer dry skin. Protects the digestive system.
Detoxifying, affects anorexia, good to fight flatulence, inflammatory
bowel disease.
Cooking time approx. 10 min
Calories p. portion: 219
1 portions
Allergens: AG

**Quantity of ingredients**
Cherry  1/8 lbs - 2oz /  50g. ()
Water  3/4 cup - 6 oz /  200g. (yes)
Wheat flakes  1/2 oz /  20g. (yes)
Banana  1/8 lbs - 2oz /  50g. (recommended)
Butter organic  1 table spoon /  10g. (little)

**Cooking instructions:**
Thoroughly wash the cherries, pluck from the stems and core. Drain the
cherries from the glass and defrost the frozen ones. Cook the cherries
with the water and the flakes in a saucepan over low heat while stirring
for about
4 minutes until the cherries are soft. Add the banana and the butter to
the porridge, finely grate with the blender.

## 9.7　Fresh full-grain porridge - from the 8th month

Regulates gastrointestinal function. Reduces Inflammation, relieves pain, detoxifying, bactericide.
Cooking time approx. 15 min
Calories p. portion: 336
1 portions
Allergens: AG

### Quantity of ingredients
Spelled wholemeal flour　1 oz /　25g. (recommended)
Cow's milk (whole milk 3.5% fat)　3/4 cup - 6 oz /　200g. ()
Honey　1 teaspoon /　3g. (little)
Banana　1 piece /　120g. (recommended)

### Cooking instructions:
Grind the cereal grains into a flour mill. You may also be able to use a coffee grinder, but then grind twice. Stir the flour with the milk in a saucepan and bring it to boil over medium heat. Cook the porridge on low heat for 4-5 minutes while stirring. Then add the honey. Crush the banana with a fork and pull it under the porridge.


## 9.8　Fruit jelly - from the 8th month

Promotes spleen and liver, reduces blood pressure, strengthens immune system. Promotes digestion. Warms stomach and spleen, improves blood circulation. For cholesterol diet.
Cooking time approx. 2 hours and more
Calories p. portion: 60
2 portions
Allergens:

### Quantity of ingredients
Carrot (Early Carrot)　3/4 lbs /　300g. (recommended)
Water　6 table spoons /　50g. (yes)
Sugar cane sugar　1 teaspoon /　3g. (little)
Gelatin white　1 Leaf /　3g. ()
Orange　1/2 piece /　50g. ()
Cinnamon ground　1 pinch /　0,2g. (yes)
Corn germ oil　1/2 teaspoon /　2g. (little)

**Cooking instructions:**
Thoroughly wash, clean, peel and slice the carrots.

Boil about 6 tablespoons of water in a saucepan, add the carrots and cane sugar and cook over medium heat for 10-15 minutes.

Meanwhile, soak the gelatin in cold water for about 10 minutes.

Squeeze the orange half, mix the juice with the cinnamon and the oil. Crush the hot carrots with the blender and dissolve the gelatin (alternative: use agar-agar) in the hot mush.

Stir in the orange juice. Swirl out a pudding mold (1/4 liter content) with cold water, pour in the carrot sauce and refrigerate in the fridge for about 3 hours.

Tip out before eating and allow to warm to room temperature.

## 9.9   Grape compote - from the 8th month

Calms stomach, strengthens tendons and bones, supports urination, promotes digestion.
Cooking time approx. 10 min
Calories p. portion: 128
1 portions
Allergens: H

**Quantity of ingredients**
Grapes red  3/8 lbs - 6oz /  150g. (yes)
Water  4 table spoons /  30g. (yes)
Almond  1 teaspoon /  3g. ()

**Cooking instructions:**
Remove the grapes from the stems, wash thoroughly in warm water and drain. Halve the grapes (remove the seeds for babies). In a small saucepan, heat 4 tablespoons of water with the grapes and the grated almonds till it  boils . Cook over low heat for about 3 minutes, then chill. (For babies lukewarm).

## 9.10 Grape juice (fresh, homemade)

Calms stomach, strengthens tendons and bones, supports urination, promotes digestion.
Cooking time approx. 15 min
Calories p. portion: 73
2 portions
Allergens:

**Quantity of ingredients**
Grapes white  7/8 lbs /  200g. (yes)

**Cooking instructions:**
For about 200 ml of juice, pluck 400 g of white grapes (alternatively berries or stone fruit) from the stalk, wash thoroughly, drain and halve. Fill in the sieve insert of the pressure cooker. On the bottom of the pot pour about 2 cm high water, stack the cross, the juice bowl (accessories) and the sieve with the grapes on top of each other. Close the pot and juice the grapes for about 12 minutes.

## 9.11 Milk mash for the bottle - from the 8th month

Little laxative. Provides Vitamin C. Diuretic, building up, eye-enhancing, detoxifying, nerve-strengthening. Nourishes and strengthens body.
Cooking time approx. 15 min
Calories p. portion: 187
1 portions
Allergens: G

**Quantity of ingredients**
Cow's milk (1.5% fat)  3/4 cup - 6 oz /  200g. ()
Millet flakes  1/2 oz /  20g. (recommended)
Pear juice  1/2 oz /  15g. ()
Orange juice  3 teaspoons /  30g. ()

**Cooking instructions:**
Mix the half of the milk in a small pot with the wholegrain flakes until smooth and heat till it boil, whisking constantly, depending on the flakes, for 2-3 minutes. Some just have to stir in the hot milk. Remove the saucepan from the heat and add the pear juice and the remaining milk while stirring. Finally, pour the orange juice through a sieve into the milk and stir well.
(For baby lukewarm cool and put in a vial).

## 9.12 Milk rice with berry juice - from the 8th month

Laxative, strengthens eyesight, good to fight chronic constipation, strengthens kidney and bladder, diuretic, warming the body from the inside, expands blood vessels, regulates internal organs functions.
Cooking time approx. 25 min
Calories p. portion: 135
1 portions
Allergens: G

### Quantity of ingredients
Raspberry  2 table spoons /  30g. (recommended)
Cow's milk (1.5% fat)  3/4 cup - 6 oz /  200g. ()
Rice mash  2 table spoons /  10g. (yes)

### Cooking instructions:
Thaw the frozen raspberries and then pass through a sieve. Mix half of the milk with the rice bran. Heat till it boils in a small saucepan and simmer over low heat while stirring for about 3 minutes. Remove the saucepan from the heat and gradually add the remaining milk and raspberry juice. Add the liquid to the bottle and shake vigorously. Depending on the season and preferences, add with fruit juices, glucose and from the 8th month, with honey or sugar cane granules.

## 9.13 Milk-free cereal fruit porridge - from the 8th month

Stops diarrhea, promotes digestion, appetizing, relieves diarrhea, strengthens immune system. Relieves pain and inflammation.
Cooking time approx. 10 min
Calories p. portion: 220
1 portions
Allergens: AG

### Quantity of ingredients
Apple (sweet)  1 piece /  100g. (recommended)
Strawberries  3 pieces /  15g. (yes)
Water  1/2 cup /  100g. (yes)
Oat flakes (whole grain)  1/2 oz /  20g. (recommended)
Butter organic  1 table spoon /  10g. (little)

**Cooking instructions:**
Wash the apple thoroughly, peel with a peeler and grate finely on an apple grater. Wash the strawberries, peel off the green and crush the berries very finely with a fork. Heat the water till it boils. Fill the flakes into a plate, pour boiling water and stir well. Then add the butter and undergo. Finally, add the grated apple and strawberries.

## 9.14 Month porridge - from 7th month

Promotes spleen and liver, strengthens immune system, improves digestion, regenerates skin, supports urination, strengthens the muscles, tendons and bones.
Cooking time approx. 2 hours and more
Calories p. portion: 157
20 portions
Allergens:

**Quantity of ingredients**
Beef soup meat  2,2 lbs /  1000g. (yes)
Water  3,3 lbs /  1400g. (yes)
Fennel seeds ground  1 teaspoon /  3g. (recommended)
Potato  50 OZ /  1500g. (recommended)
Carrot (Early Carrot)  7 lbs /  3000g. (recommended)

**Cooking instructions:**
Wash the beef and place in the pressure cooker with about 1/2 liter of water.
Add the fennel seeds, close the pot and put it on. Cook at level 1 in about 45 minutes. Then remove from the heat and wait until the pressure has dropped. (Cook in a normal saucepan for approx. 1 ½ hours) In the meantime, wash the potatoes and place them in a saucepan without peeling. Add about 5 cm of water, bring to the boil and cook the potatoes on a low heat for 35-40 minutes. Remove the meat from the broth and cut into cubes of about 2 cm. Wash, clean, peel and divide the carrots into large pieces. Cook half of the carrots in a closed pot on level 1 in about 6 minutes. Let evaporate and lift the carrots out with a slotted spoon. Then cook the remaining carrots. In a bowl, finely puree the meat with carrots and 1 trowel of bouillon with the blender until everything is chopped up. Peel the still hot potatoes and press in portions through the potato press. Do not crush with blenders - then the puree becomes paste-like. Mix the loose potato puree with the carrot and meat sauce. In freezer bags, weigh 190-220 g portions (depending on age and appetite), seal and freeze in the freezer.

The porridge is stable for up to 2 months. If necessary, thaw the bag and its contents in warm water. Bring the vegetables to the boil and mix on the plate with 1 tablespoon of butter or germ oil (change daily). Add the fat after cooking - otherwise important vitamins and fatty acids will be destroyed!

## 9.15 Peach mash uncooked - from the 8th month

Supports erythrocyte production, relieves fatigue, relaxes. Protects the digestive system. Detoxifying, affects anorexia, good to fight flatulence, inflammatory bowel disease.
Cooking time approx. 10 min
Calories p. portion: 191
1 portions
Allergens: AG

### Quantity of ingredients
Water  1/2 cup /  100g. (yes)
Wheat flakes  1/2 oz /  20g. (yes)
Butter organic  1 table spoon /  10g. (little)
Peaches  1 piece /  120g. (yes)

### Cooking instructions:
Boil the water once, stir in the flakes. Add the butter. Wash the peach very thoroughly, douse in a small bowl with boiling hot water. Leave the peach in it for about 2 minutes until the peel peels off easily. Skin the peach, cut it into quarters and remove it from the core. Mince the pulp with the blender. Mix the peaches under the mash and fill in a plate.

## 9.16 Porridge with apple - from the 8th month

Stops diarrhea, promotes digestion, appetizing, relieves diarrhea, strengthens immune system.
Cooking time approx. 15 min
Calories p. portion: 279
1 portions
Allergens: AG

### Quantity of ingredients
Cow's milk (whole milk 3.5% fat)  3/4 cup - 6 oz /  200g. ()
Oat flakes (whole grain)  2 table spoons /  20g. (recommended)
Apple (sweet)  1 piece /  120g. (recommended)

**Cooking instructions:**
Heat the milk with the oatmeal in a small saucepan till it boils. After about 1 minute, pull in front of the hotplate and let it rest for 3-4 minutes, covered. Wash the apple thoroughly under running water, rub dry and peel. Rub on an apple grater and stir it under the oatmeal and fill everything into a plate.

## 9.17 Puréed banana

Eat 2 times a day, regulates gastrointestinal function
Cooking time approx. 7 min
Calories p. portion: 144
1 portions
Allergens:

**Quantity of ingredients**
Banana  1 piece /  150g. (recommended)

**Cooking instructions:**
Mix the banana with the fork or purée with a blender. Leave to brown for at least 5 minutes.

## 9.18 Rusk, milk and carrot puree - from the 8th month

Promotes spleen and liver, reduces blood pressure, strengthens immune system. Protects the digestive system. Detoxifying, affects anorexia, good to fight flatulence, inflammatory bowel disease. Little laxative.
Cooking time approx. 10 min
Calories p. portion: 112
1 portions
Allergens: AG

**Quantity of ingredients**
Carrot (Early Carrot)  1 oz /  30g. (recommended)
Water  2 table spoons /  0g. (yes)
Cow's milk (1.5% fat)  3/4 cup - 6 oz /  200g. ()
Rusk  3 slices /  4g. (recommended)

**Cooking instructions:**
Wash the carrot, peel and cut into small pieces. Cook in a small saucepan with the water for about 10 minutes until soft. Then puree. Heat the milk in a pot. Place the rusks in a cloth napkin, grasp the napkin at the four ends and twist together. Crush the rusks with a potato

masher, place in a plate. Pour half of the hot milk over it, let it stand for about 1 minute. Then mix the porridge with the carrot sauce. Allow the remaining milk to cool slightly and pour it into the bottle, feed to it.

## 9.19 Semolina mash with grape puree - from the 8th month

Protects the digestive system. Affects anorexia, good to fight flatulence, inflammatory bowel disease. Strengthens tendons and bones, supports urination, promotes digestion. Little laxative.
Cooking time approx. 10 min
Calories p. portion: 204
1 portions
Allergens: AG

### Quantity of ingredients
Grapes white  6 pieces /  15g. (yes)
Cow's milk (1.5% fat)  3/4 cup - 6 oz /  200g. ()
Wheat semolina for children  2 table spoons /  30g. (recommended)

### Cooking instructions:
Wash the grapes, cut in half, remove the peel and remove the seeds. Finely chop the pulp, collecting the juice. Heat half of the milk. Add the semolina (not whole wheat), heat till it boils and simmer over low heat with stirring in about 3 minutes. Remove the pot from the cooking area and gradually add the remaining milk and the grape marc.
You can easily sweeten semolina pudding with fruit purée or fruit juice.

## 9.20 Spring vegetables - from the 8th month

Diuretic, supports urination, supports digestion. Diuretic, harmonizes the stomach and intestines, conducts bowel winds, strengthens immune system.
Cooking time approx. 1 1/2 hour
Calories p. portion: 64
8 portions
Allergens: G

### Quantity of ingredients
Carrot  1,1 lbs /  500g. (recommended)
Kohlrabi  1,1 lbs /  500g. ()
Butter organic  2 table spoons /  20g. (little)
Water  1/2 cup /  125g. (yes)

**Cooking instructions:**

Wash the vegetables thoroughly. Clean and peel carrots and turnip cabbage. From the turnip cabbage, finely chop some delicate leaves and set aside. Rasp the carrots and the turnip cabbage. Melt the butter, add the water and the vegetables and cook over medium heat for about 30 minutes. Stir occasionally. Spread the vegetables and cooked water to about 8 deep-frozen bags to a100-150 g (depending on the age of the child). Close the bags, allow them to cool down and freeze them for max 3 months.

If necessary thaw, boil and mix with 80g of boiled potatoes and an egg. (The recipe can easily be varied if you want to use cauliflower, peas or zucchini)

## 9.21 Tender fennel vegetables - from 6th month

Relieves constipation, stimulates nerves, reduces inflammation, improves blood circulation, regenerates skin, supports urination. Promotes digestion.
Cooking time approx. 25 min
Calories p. portion: 70
2 portions
Allergens: G

**Quantity of ingredients**

Potato  1 piece /  50g. (recommended)
Fennel  1/4 lbs - 4oz /  100g. (recommended)
Water  2 table spoons /  20g. (yes)
Butter organic  1 table spoon /  10g. (little)

**Cooking instructions:**

Wash the potato and peel with a peeler. Cut into cubes of about 2 cm. Wash the fennel, remove stained, dark spots and cut the tuber. Heat till it boils with 2 tablespoons of water in a small saucepan. Cook on low heat for about 15 minutes. Fish out the caraway seeds. Puree the vegetables with the blender and stir in the butter.

Fennel and caraway soothe the stomach and prevent bloating. In addition, fennel contains a lot of vitamin C and folic acid. An ideal meal for sick children.

## 9.22 Vegetable porridge - from the 6th month

Promotes spleen and liver, strengthens immune system. Improves digestion. Strengthens bone marrow.
Cooking time approx. 20 min
Calories p. portion: 161
1 portions
Allergens: G

### Quantity of ingredients
Potato  1 piece /  50g. (recommended)
Carrot (Early Carrot) 1/4 lbs - 4oz /  100g. (recommended)
Chicken meat  1 oz /  30g. (recommended)
Butter organic  1 table spoon /  10g. (little)

### Cooking instructions:
Wash the potato and put it unpeeled in a small pot. Cover with a little water and bring to boil, then cook the potatoes on a low heat for 15-20 minutes.
Meanwhile, wash the carrots, clean, peel and cut into pieces about 2 cm in size. Steam with 3 tablespoons of water and the meat in a pot for about 15 minutes.
Finely chop the carrots and meat with a blencer. Add the butter and puree everything.
(Change again and again the vegetables: kohlrabi, zucchini, parsnips)

## 9.23 Vegetable potato and meat mash - from 10th month

Strengthens immune system, reduces inflammation, improves digestion, strengthens spleen and stomach, strengthens the muscles, tendons and bones, antiparasitic.
Cooking time approx. 30 min
Calories p. portion: 127
2 portions
Allergens:

### Quantity of ingredients
Potato  1/4 lbs - 4oz /  100g. (recommended)
Carrot (Early Carrot)  5/8 oz /  200g. (recommended)
Beef meat (calf)  1/8 lbs - 2oz /  40g. (recommended)
Apricots juice  6 table spoons /  60g. (little)
Rapeseed oil  1 table spoon /  6g. (little)

**Cooking instructions:**
Remove the flesh, skin, tendons and grease, wash under cool water and cut into small pieces and boil in a little water. After about 15-20 minutes, remove and puree. Wash the vegetables and potatoes, peel and cut into not too small pieces. Cook gently with a little water over a low heat for 10-20 minutes. Use the blender to chop the vegetables. Mix everything, add butter or oil and fruit juice and puree again.
Alternately use other meats such as chicken, lamb or turkey. Also change vegetables with zucchini, kohlrabi, fennel, pumpkin, parsnips and broccoli.
Also change the fruit juices. This can produce a variety of flavors.

## 9.24 Vegetarian Vegetable Porridge - from the 8th month

Stops diarrhea, promotes digestion, appetizing, relieves diarrhea, promotes spleen and liver, strengthens immune system, provides vitamin C. Diuretic, building up, eye-enhancing, Detoxifying, nerve-strengthening.
Cooking time approx. 20 min
Calories p. portion: 261
1 portions
Allergens: C

**Quantity of ingredients**
Carrot (Early Carrot)  1/4 lbs - 4oz /  100g. (recommended)
Millet flakes  1/2 oz /  20g. (recommended)
Chicken yolk  1 piece /  20g. ()
Orange juice  2 table spoons /  20g. ()
Apple (sweet)  1 piece /  100g. (recommended)
Corn germ oil  1 teaspoon /  3g. (little)

**Cooking instructions:**
Wash, peel and chop the carrots. Boil in 150 ml of water. Cook on low heat for 15 minutes. Sprinkle the millet flakes and add the egg yolks. Heat the porridge till it boils while stirring constantly and remove from heat.
Wash, peel and chop the apple. Pour the orange juice into the porridge and finely chop it with the blender. Pour the porridge into a plate, add the butter or the oil and stir well.
(Only 1 egg yolk per week, otherwise increase the amount of fat to 1 tablespoon of butter or oil.)

## 9.25 Vegetarian vegetable-oatmeal-potatoes mash

Improves digestion, regenerates skin, supports urination, lowers cholesterol, supports urination, relieves constipation, strengthens mother milk production.
Cooking time approx. 25 min
Calories p. portion: 91
2 portions
Allergens: A

### Quantity of ingredients
Carrot (Early Carrot)  1 oz /  30g. (recommended)
Parsnip  1 oz /  30g. (yes)
Zucchini  1 oz /  30g. (recommended)
Fennel  1/2 oz /  10g. (recommended)
Potato  1/8 lbs - 2oz /  50g. (recommended)
Water  1/2 oz /  20g. (yes)
Oat flakes (whole grain)  1/2 oz /  10g. (recommended)
Orange juice  1 oz /  30g. ()
Rapeseed oil  1/4 oz /  8g. (little)

### Cooking instructions:
Wash the vegetables and potatoes, dice and fry in a little water. Add water and oatmeal, puree everything and finally add the oil. Note: This porridge replaces the vegetable-potato-meat porridge when meat is to be dispensed with in the infant's diet. Since meat is the best food source for iron, a vegetarian diet must pay particular attention to a sufficient supply of iron.

## 9.26 Whole milk cereal mash - from the 8th month

Reduces Inflammation, antiallergic, has a stabilizing effect on the blood circulation, lowers blood glucose and cholesterol.
Cooking time approx. 20 min
Calories p. portion: 205
1 portions
Allergens: AG

### Quantity of ingredients
Cow's milk (whole milk 3.5% fat)  3/4 cup - 6 oz /  200g. ()
Water  1/4 cup /  50g. (yes)
Spelled flakes  1/2 oz /  20g. (recommended)
Fruit mix juice  1/2 oz /  20g. (little)

**Cooking instructions:**
Boil the milk with the wholegrain flakes and let it swell. Add the pureed fruit.

Switch between wheat, oats and wholemeal spelled flakes, as well as the fruits. So you get a variety of flavors.

# 10 Effects of food

## 10.1 Use ingredients: recommendable

Acai powder
Anise (Common Fennel)
Apple (sweet)
Apple puree
Apricot
Aubergine
Avocado
Banana
Banchatee (green tea)
Barley grass powder
Barley malt
Bay leaf
Bearberry leaf
Beef meat
Beef meat (calf)
Berries of the season
Bitter Herb liqueur
Black caraway
Blackberry´s
Blueberry
Borage
Broccoli
Cantaloupe
Carrot
Carrot (Early Carrot)
Carrot juice without sugar
Cauliflower
Chamomile tea
Channa-Dal
Chenpi (chinese tangerine bowl)
Chicken meat
Coix (seeds) YiYi Ren
Compote (fruits of the season)
Corn
Corn (fast polenta)
Corn flour
Corn Grease (Polenta)
Cream 10% coffee cream
Cucumber
Dashi
Dill
Elderberries
Fennel
Fennel seeds ground
Fennel tea

Fox nut, gorgon nut, makhana
Gentian root
Gentian root tea
Gourd
Ground
Ground caraway
Herbal tea mix
Hibiscus
Hokkaido pumpkin
Kudzu
Lily bulbs
Lime blossom tea
Lovage
Mascarpone cheese
Millet
Millet flakes
Oat
Oat flakes (whole grain)
Oat flakes roasted
Oat flour
Oat fusion (baby food)
Papaya
Parsley root
Pear
Potato
Potato (mealy)
Pumpkin
Raspberry
Rusk
Spelled (Dark) bread
Spelled flakes
Spelled grain
Spelled semolina
Spelled wholemeal flour
Spinach
Sugar fructose - fruit sugar
Sugar glucose - grapes sugar
Sugar Milk Sugar
Turkey breast meat
Wakame
Watermelon
Wax gourd
Wheat semolina for children
Yogi tea
Zucchini

## 10.2 Use ingredients: yes

Amaranth

Apple (sour)

Arrowroot
Asparagus (green or white)
Balm
Banana (cooking banana)
Barley
Barley flour
Barley grouts
Barley not peeled
Basic recipe for a beef soup
Basic recipe for a beef soup (warming)
Basic recipe for a chicken soup
(warming)
Basic recipe for a rice soup (Congee)
Basic recipe for a vegetable soup
(nutritious)
Basil
Basil (fresh)
Batavia
Beef fillet
Beef meatbones
Beef soup meat
Blackthorn (Sloe)
Blue mallow tee
Bread roll
Bread with carob kernel flour
Breadcrumbs (wheat bread, bread roll)
Bulgur (cereals)
Burdock root tea
Cardamom
Carob flour, St. john's bread
Celery root
Celery sticks
Chamomile
Chard
Chervil
Chervil dried
Cinnamon ground
Cinnamon sticks
Clove
Coriander
Coriander (fresh)
Corn silk tea
Corn starch
Couscous
Cranberries
Cranberry
Cranberry
Cranberry juice
Cress
Currant (black)
Currant (red)
Currant (white)
Dandelion (young plants)

Dandelion juice
Dates red
Elderberry blossom tee
Fig
Fruit tea
Goat
Gooseberry
Grapes red
Grapes white
Hawthorn
Herbs of Provence
Herbs various
Herbs wild
Hibiscus tea
Hyssop
Jasmine blossoms tee
Juniper berry
King Solomon's-seal
Ladyfingers
Lamb bones
Lamb meat
Lamb shoulder
Lavender blossoms
Lemon Balm (dried)
Lemon Balm (fresh)
Lemongrass
Licorice root tea
Liver smoothing tea
Lovage seeds
Lye roll
Mallow (Malva sylvestris) blossom tea
Margarine
Margarine (diet)
Marjoram
Mulberry fruit
Multi-grain bread (gray bread)
Mutton
Mutton
Nasturtium (nose-twister or nose-
tweaker)
Noodles (wheat) with egg
Noodles (wheat, lasagne) with egg
Noodles (wheat, ribbon noodles) with
egg
Nutmeg
Oat meal
Oat milk
Oregano fresh
Palm oil
Parsley
Parsnip
Passion blossoms tea
Passion fruit
Peaches

Peaches (canned)
Pearl barley
Pearl barley
Peppermint
Peppermint tea
Peppers
Pigeon
Pork ham
Pork ham cooked
Pork ham smoked
Pork knuckle
Pork meat
Potato flour
Pudding powder vanilla
Quail
Quince
Quinoa
Rabbit
Rabbit (wild)
Rabbit meat
Radish (white, green, purple-red)
Radish black
Radish leaves
Raspberry leaf tea
Red beet
Red berry (without sugar)
Rhubarb
Ribworttea
Rice (fragrance)
Rice (Gaoliang / Sorghum)
Rice Basmati
Rice flour
Rice long grain rice
Rice malt
Rice mash
Rice noodles
Rice red
Rice round grain
Rice starch
Rice sticky
Rice sweet
Rice variety any
Rose blossom tea
Rose hip tea
Rose leaf tea
Rosemary
Rye

Rye flour
Saffron
Sage
Sago (cereals)
Salsify
Sea buckthorn
Sorrel
Sourdough
Soy flour
Soy noodles
Star anise
Strawberries
Sweet potato
Thyme
Thyme dried
Tomato
Tomato paste
Tomato puree
Topinambur
Tsampa (roasted barley flour)
Turkey ham
Turnip
Turnips
Valerian
Vanilla
Vanilla pod
Vanilla powder
Vegetable juice
Water
Water hot
Wheat
Wheat bulgur
Wheat flakes
Wheat flatbread/pita bread
Wheat flour
Wheat semolina
White bread (baguette)
White bread (roll)
White bread (wheat bread)
White breadcrumbs
White dumpling bread (wheat bread cut into chunks)
Wild strawberries
Yam root, yam root tuber
Yarrow
Yarrow tea

## 10.3 Use ingredients: little

Apple juice (natural cloudy)
Apricot jam
Apricots

Apricots juice
Blackberry jam
Blueberry dried

Blueberry jam
Blueberry juice
Butter (half fat)
Butter organic
Chives
Corn germ oil
Cranberry jam
Currant jam (black)
Currant jam (red)
Currant juice (black)
Fructose (glucose)
Fruit mix juice
Grape juice red
Grape juice white
Grapeseed oil
Honey
Leek
Linseed oil
Mango
Mango juice
Manioc flour
Mirabelle plum
Mustard seeds
Nectarine
Noodles (whole grain) with egg
Olive oil
Plum
Plums
Pumpkin seed oil
Radish

Radish horseradish
Rapeseed oil
Raspberry jam
Rice (whole grain)
Rice black
Rice wild (nature rice)
Sesame oil
Sesame oil roasted
Sour cherries
Soybean oil
Strawberry jam
Sugar - icing sugar
Sugar brown
Sugar candy white
Sugar cane sugar
Sugar molasses
Sugar palm sugar
Sugar white
Sunflower oil
Toast bread (whole grain)
Tomato juice
Umeboshi plums (Japanese apricots)
Vanilla sugar natural
Walnut oil
Wheat flour whole grain
Wheat germ oil
Wheat/Rye/Gray-black bread with yeast
Whole grain bread
Wholemeal flour
Wild garlic (garlic spinach)

## 10.4 Do not use contra-acting foods

Acerola fruit nectar or powder
Adzuki beans
Agar agar (kelp)
Agave nectar
Agrimony
Almond
Almond marzipan
Almond milk
Almond puree
Aloe juice
Amaranth Pops
Anchovy / Sardine
Angelica root
Apricot dried
Apricot nectar
Artichoke
Baking powder
Bamboo shoots
barberry
Basic recipe for a duck soup
Basic recipe for a fish soup

Bean oil
Beans (green, fresh)
Beef bone marrow
Beef heart
Beef heart (calf)
Beef kidney
Beef liver
Beef lungs (calf)
Beef Oxtail pieces
Beef stomach
Beer (alcohol-free)
Beer (alcohol-reduced)
Beer (Pils)
Beer (Top-fermented German dark beer)
Berry juice
Bitter Lemon
Bitter liqueur
Bitter orange peel
Black beans
Black fungus mushroom

Black tea
Blackberry dried (unripe fruit)
Blackberry leaves
Black-eyed peas
Bocksdorn fruits (Fructus Lycii, Goji, goji berry
Boletus mushroom
Borage oil
Boxhorn clover seeds
Brazil nuts
Brie cheese
Broad beans (thick beans)
Brown ale
Brussels sprouts
Buckbean
Buckwheat
Buckwheat (roasted) Kasha
Buckwheat whole grain
Bush beans
Butter beans white
Buttermilk
Calamari
Camembert
Campari
Capers in olive oil
Carambola (Star fruit)
Carp
Cashews
Caviar
Cereal coffee
Champignon
Chanterelle
Cherry
Cherry (sour)
Cherry compote
Cherry juice
Chestnut puree
Chestnuts
Chicken Blood
Chicken egg
Chicken egg white
Chicken heart
Chicken liver
Chicken stomach
Chicken yolk
Chickpeas
Chickweed
Chicory
Chili (pod or ground)
Chinese cabbage
Chinese pearl barley
Chlorella (fresh water)
Chocolate
Chocolate (Diabetic)

Chrysanthemum blossom tea
Clarified butter
Clementine
Clementines
Cocoa
Coconut fat
Coconut flakes
Coconut grated
Coconut meat
Coconut milk
Cod
Codfish
Coffee
Cola drink
Cola drink (low calorie)
Cooking oil
Corn (roasted)
Cottage cheese
Cow's milk (1.5% fat)
Cow's milk (whole milk 3.5% fat)
Crab
Cream (30% fat)
Cream sour 10%
Cream sour 20%
Cream sour 30%
Cream, sweet 30%
Creamer
Créme fraiche cheese
Crispbread
Crucian
Cucumber (bitter)
Cucumber (spicy cucumber)
Cumin (Caraway seed)
Curcuma
Curd cheese 20%
Curd cheese 40%
Currants (black)
Currants (red)
Curry
Curry paste red
Daisy
Dandelionroots tea
Dates dried
Deer meat
Deer meat
Deer's Bones
Deer's kidneys
Duck (heart)
Duck (slaughtered)
Ducks egg
Dulse (seaweed)
Dyer's broom herb
Edam cheese
Eel

Eel smoked
Emmental cheese
Endive salad
Evening primrose oil
Fenugreek (Trigonella foenum-graecum)
Fernet Branca (herbal bitter liqueur)
Feta cheese
Feta cheese
Fig dried
Fish innards
Fish pieces mixed (fresh water)
Fish remains
Fish sauce
Flounder
Flower pollen
French beans
Fresh cheese
Fresh cheese from soya
Fresh cheese with herbs
Freshwater crab
Freshwater fish
Gail plum
Galangal
Garam Masala powder
Garlic
Gelatin white
Gelee Royal
Ginger fresh
Ginger oil
Ginger powder
Ginkgo fruit
Ginseng
Ginseng liqueur
Ginseng root
Goat and sheep's blood
Goat and sheep's brain
Goat and sheep's liver
Goat and sheep's milk
Goat and sheep's stomach
Goat cheese
Goose
Goose blood
Goose egg
Goose fat
Goose parts
Gorgonzola
Gouda cheese
Grapefruit (Pomelo)
Grapefruit dried peel
Grapefruit juice
Grass carp
Green spelt
Green tea

Greengage
Guava
Halibut (Flatfish)
Hazelnuts
Herbs bitter
Herring
Hijiki
Honey wine (Met)
Hop
Horehound leaves
Horse meat
Iceberg lettuce
Jellyfish
Kaki plum
Kalmus
Kefir
Kidney beans (red)
Kiwi
Kohlrabi
Kombu seaweed (Saccharina japonica)
Kukicha tea
Kumquats
Lamb kidneys
Lamb liver
Lamb's lettuce
Lamb's lettuce
Leaf salads (bitter)
Lemon
Lemon juice
Lemon peel
Lentils
Lentils black
Lentils red
Lentils yellow
Lettuce
Lima beans
Lime
Linseed
Linseed (crushed)
Lobster
Longane
Loquate / Japanese medlar
Lotus roots
Lotus seeds
Luo Han Guo fruit
Lychee
Lychee in Preserved
Lychee liqueur
Mackerel
Malt
Maple syrup
Mare's milk
Martini
Mayonnaise 50%

Mayonnaise 80%
Mediterranean fish (cod, plaice, haddock, sea
Medlar
Mineral water
Miso
Miso black (fermented)
Miso paste (soy bean paste)
Mixed Pickles
Mold cheese
Morel (black, dried)
Morel, dried
Mozzarella
Mu Erh Mushroom
Muesli
Mulled Wine Spice
Mullet
Mung bean
Mung bean sprouting
Mussels
Mustard
Mustard Dijon
Mustard medium hot
Mustard sweet
Nettles
Noodles (wheat, spaghetti) with egg
Nori, purple seaweed, red algae
Octopus
Octopus
Okra
Olives
Olives green
Onion (shallot)
Onion (spring onion)
Onion read
Onion white
Orange
Orange blossom
Orange dried peel
Orange grated peel
Orange jam
Orange juice
Orange peel
Oregano dried
Oyster mushroom
Oyster shell powder
Oysters
Parmesan
Peanut (roasted)
Peanut butter
Peanut oil
Peanuts
Pear juice
Peas

Peas, green
Pepper (ground)
Pepper Cayenne
Pepper powder (hot)
Pepper white (ground)
Peppercorns
Pepperoni
Pepperoni, red, pitted, halved
Pepperoni, yellow, pitted, halved
Peppers (rose peppers)
Peppers (sweet)
Peppers powder
Perch
Pheasant
Pickle
Pig blood
Pigeon egg
Pimento
Pine nuts
Pineapple
Pineapple (from a can)
Pineapple juice without sugar
Pinto beans speckled
Pistachios
Plaice
Plum dried
Pomegranate
Poppy
Pork Bacon
Pork brain
Pork fat (lard)
Pork heart
Pork kidneys
Pork Lard
Pork liver
Pork lung
Pork marrow bones
Pork sausage (Bratwurst)
Pork skin
Pork stomach
Pork/beef sausage (smoked)
Pork's intestine
Prickly pear
Processed cheese 12%
processed cheese 30%
Prosecco
Psyllium seed
Puff pastry
Pumpernickel (dark bread)
Pumpkin seeds
Quail egg
Rabbit liver
Radicchio
Ra sins

Raspberry dried (immature)
Red cabbage
Red wine
Reishi mushroom
Romaine lettuce / lettuce salad
Rose hip
Rosefish
Rucola
Rum
Rye wholemeal bread
Safflower (Dyer's thistle / Hong Hua)
Sake
Salmon
Salt
Salt (herbal)
Sauerkraut (cutted cabbage fermented)
Savory
Savoy cabbage / kale
Sea cucumber
Seacrab
Sesame paste (Tahini)
Sesame, black
Sesame, white
Shark
Sheep's milk
Sheep's milk yoghurt
Sherry (whine)
Shiitake, dried
Shrimp
Shrimps
Skim milk powder
Slug
Sour cream 15% fat
Sour milk
Sour milk cheese 20%
Soy sauce
Soy Tofu
Soy Tofu smoked
Soya Cuisine (soy cream)
Soybean milk
Soybeans
Soybeans, black
Soybeans, blacks, fermented
Soybeans, yellow
Spiny lobsters
Spirit

Spurdog (spiny dogfish, Schillerlocken)
St. Benedict's thistle, blessed thistle,
holy thistle,
Stevia (candyleaf, sweetleaf)
Strawberry Juice
Sugar substitute (sweetener)
Sunflower seeds
Supplementary nutrition
Tabasco
Tangerine
Tarragon (Estragon)
Tea mixture uric acid lowering
Thistle oil
Tomato dried
Tonic Water
Trout
Trout (smoked)
Truffle
Tuna
Turmeric (yellow root)
Umeboshi paste
Vinegar (Apple vinegar)
Vinegar (Red wine vinegar)
Vinegar Aceto Balsamico
Vinegar Aceto Balsamico white
Walnuts
Walnuts roasted
Wheat beer
Wheat bran
Wheatgrass juice
Wheatgrass powder
Whey
White beans
White bread (pretzel sticks)
White cabbage
White wine
Whitefish
Wild boar meat
Wild herbs
Wormwood
Wormwood herb
Yeast
Yew nut
Yoghurt vanilla
Yogurt (natural, 1.5% fat)
Yogurt (natural, 3.5% fat)

# 11  Herbs and their effects

## 11.1  Basil

It has a beneficial effect on flatulence and nausea, relaxing and soothing. Good to fight emphysema, bronchitis, whooping cough, high blood pressure, headache, mouth odor, warts, hiccup, gout, migraine.

## 11.2  Lovage

Stimulates digestion, reduces pain. Extracts of the root are used to flush out urinary tract infections and prevent kidney gravel.

## 11.3  Parsley

Stimulates liver function, detoxifies. Forces urinating. Relieves flatulence. Digestive and menstrual stimulating, birth-accelerating, memory-enhancing, blood-purifying, skin-smoothing.

## 11.4  Thyme dried

Disinfecting. It stimulates the blood circulation, increases the appetite and helps to digest fat meat better. Strengthens lungs and spleen (TCM).

# 12 Basics of Nutrition

The basic principles of nutrition described herein are general recommendations. They are not aimed at a specific form of therapy. Recommendations concerning a therapy have priority.

## 12.1 Nutrition

Regular meals in a relaxed atmosphere. A warm breakfast is considered a good start into the day.
The main meals ought to be taken for lunch – supper in the early evening. Pay attention to feeling hungry or sated: don't eat too much nor remain hungry is the rule
Prepare the meals freshly from natural, regional products. Frozen, heat-conserved, industrially prepared or foodstuffs cooked in the microwave oven are rejected.
Choice of foodstuffs according to the season: more cooling food in summer, more warming food in winter.
Eat cooked food at least twice a day. Food and drinks ought to be lukewarm, never ice-cold or hot.
Raw vegetables, briefly cooked vegetables, freshly squeezed juices and mineral water are not recommended. Milk and dairy products are only included in the diet if they don't cause problems.
Don't use therapeutic recipes over a longer period without consulting your doctor or therapist.

**Varied food**
Enjoy the diversity of foodstuffs. Characteristics of a balanced nutrition are variety, suitable combination and a balanced quantity of rich and low energy foodstuffs (on one hand avoiding undersupply with essential nutrients and on the other hand to take to many undesirable substances).

**A lot of Cereal Products - and Potatoes**
Bread, pasta, rice, cereal flakes (best wholemeal) as well as potatoes contain almost no fat, but many vitamins, mineral nutrients, trace elements, roughage and secondary plant substances. These foodstuffs ought to be taken with low-fat side dishes.

**Vegetables and Fruit – „Take Five" every day …**
5 portions of vegetables and fruit a day, as fresh as possible, briefly cooked, or maybe one portion as a juice – ideal as a side dish to every meal as well as snack between meals: Thus a lot of vitamins, mineral nutrients as well as roughage and secondary plant substances

## Daily milk and dairy products
Milk and Dairy Products every Day, once or twice per Week Fish; meat, sausages as well as eggs moderately. These foodstuffs contain valuable nutrients like calcium in the milk, iodine selenium and omega-3 fat acids in saltwater fish. Meat is favorable due to its high content of disposable iron and the vitamins B1, B6 and B12. Quantities of 300 – 600 g meat and sausage per week are sufficient. Prefer low-fat products, especially in meat- and dairy products.

## Low-fat and fatty Foodstuffs
Fat supplies us with essential fat acids and fatty foodstuffs contain also fat-soluble vitamins. Fat is high in energy; therefore much fat in the food may cause overweight, possibly also cancer. Too many saturated fat acids may further a tendency for cardio-vascular diseases in the long term. Prefer vegetable oils and fats (e.g. rapeseed-, olive-, soya-oils and solid fats produced therefrom). Beware of invisible fat in meat- and dairy products, pastry and sweets as well as in fast-food and convenience foods. 70 – 90 g fat per day is sufficient.

## Moderately Sugar and Salt
Take sugar and foods/drinks containing various kinds of sugar (e.g. glucose syrup) only occasionally. Use herbs and spices as well as a little salt creatively. Prefer salt containing iodine.

## Plenty of Liquids
Water is absolutely essential. Drink 1-2 l liquids every day. Prefer water (with or without gas) and other low-calorie drinks. Alcoholic drinks should not be taken.

## Tasty Dishes, carefully cooked
Cook the meals with as low temperatures and as short as possible, using little water and fat – this preserves the original taste, keeps the nutrients intact and prevents the production of harmful compounds.

## Take time and enjoy the food
Take your Time and enjoy your Food
Eating consciously helps to eat right. The eye enjoys food, too. It's fun, invites to enjoy varied dishes and stimulates the feeling of satiety.

## Watch your Weight and stay in Motion
A balanced diet and a lot of exercise and sport (30 – 60 min/day) are a healthy combination. The right weight furthers well-being and health. Thermals, directional effectiveness, digestive power

There are various criteria for judging the effectiveness of herbs and foodstuffs.

The use of certain herbs and ingredients is based on observations of the effects on the body which these foodstuffs, herbs and spices show after having eaten them. The medical science has developed following system: Every ingredient or herb has a directional effectiveness. Furthermore, there are herbs which have a special effect on certain organs.

The basic condition for a healthy metabolism is to obtain sufficient energy from food and that the digestive process doesn't use too much energy. An easily digestible meal makes content and sated, doesn't cause flatulence and fatigue after the meal. The perfect spices increase the healthiness of our meals. Very often, just small doses of herbs and spices will suffice. They are not used to make us sated, but to help our digestive organs to digest the food.

## 12.2 Recipes

The recipes list the ingredients to be used and the cooking instructions show how the dish is prepared. The list of ingredients shows the concerned quantities as well as the relevance for the therapy. If you find „less than mentioned", try to comply or find an alternative from the „list of recommended foodstuffs". Mostly it shall result just in a small change of taste when you simply avoid this ingredient.

Mild cooking methods: boiling, stewing, poaching, steaming
Strong cooking methods: barbecuing, roasting, frying, smoking
Balanced cooking methods: deep-frying, baking brick
Deep-freezing and warming in the microwave oven should be avoided (denaturalization).

## 12.3 Foodstuffs

Foodstuffs have an effect on body and soul like medicinal herbs, only a very much milder one. Dietary advice is mainly based on regional foodstuffs. The knowledge about the effects of each foodstuff and the knowledge, when which foodstuff shall be used, is based on the orthodox school of medicine. Use ecologic-organic products, if possible. As everything should be cooked for a long time due to a better digestability and very rarely eaten raw, the food agrees with everyone.

The classification of the foodstuffs according to their effect on the body is the basis in order to achieve a harmonious status of health.

Dietary advisors do not recommend certain foodstuffs for everyone. The individual diet is tailor-made for the individual constitution.

Buy only fresh and ripe fruit and vegetables. You ought to leave unripe fruit and vegetables and such with brown spots and wilted leaves behind in the market. In this case take deep-frozen goods (never ready-to-serve dishes!). Fruit and vegetables are deep-frozen immediately after harvesting and often contain more vitamins and minerals than the goods from the vegetable shelf. Whereas conserved or tinned goods contain very much less biological substances. Also, salt, sugar and others are mostly added to the latter. Never leave the foodstuffs in the water after washing them to avoid that many vital substances get drowned. Clean salads, fruit and vegetables immediately before serving.

Please make sure of the hygienic processing of foodstuffs. Clean your salads, fruit and vegetables carefully. When cooking with meat, prepare all ingredients first and then process the meat products. Clean the worktop and tools very carefully. Wooden surfaces ought to be treated with a mild disinfectant regularly in order to reduce germination.

Store fruit and vegetables separately, if possible. Harvested fruit and vegetables are still alive and emit e.g. ethylene gas, which makes other products ripen and age faster. Keep meat and fish in the closed packaging or store them in the fridge in closed containers.

## 12.4 Herbs

There are some basic rules for storing medicinal herbs. On principle, herbs must be protected from direct sunlight, humidity and heat.

Containers for the storage of herbs may be glasses, ceramic jars and even plastic containers. However, plastic is a rather unsuitable material and should only be a short-term solution. In case of glass containers, use a dark material.

Medicinal herbs cannot be kept for any long period. The shelf life of herbs is limited. However, it can be prolonged with suitable storage. The place should be dark, rather cool and absolutely dry. A wooden medicine cabinet, placed not directly next to a source of heat, would be ideal. Never buy large quantities of herbs so as not to have to throw them away. Label the container with the name of the herb and the date of harvesting or processing.

# 13 Other dietic-books

The following syndromes of dietetics, TCM or for a therapy supplement for cancer are available.

## <u>Dietetics</u>

E001. Nutrition of the infant - baby food
E002. Nutrition during lactation
E003. Nutrition in old age
E004. Nutrition of children and adolescents
E005. Nutrition of athletes
E006. Light weight
E007. Pregnancy
E008. Full food

### Protein and electrolyte - kidneys
E009. (hemodialysis) dialysis treatment
E010. Acute renal failure
E011. Chronic renal insufficiency
E012. Nephrotic syndrome
E013. Kidney stones (nephrolithiasis)

### Gastrointestinal tract - pancreas
E014. Acute pancreatitis (inflammation of the pancreas)
E015. Chronic pancreatitis (inflammation of the pancreas)

### Gastrointestinal tract - small intestine and large intestine
E016. Acute obstipation (constipation)
E017. Chronic obstipation (constipation)
E018. Colon irritabile
E019. Diverticulitis
E020. Acquired lactose intolerance (lactose malabsorption)
E021. Fructose malabsorption
E022. Glutensensitive enteropathy (celiac disease)
E023. Colectomy
E024. Short Bowel Syndrome

### Gastrointestinal tract - liver, gallbladder, bile ducts
E025. Acute and chronic hepatitis (inflammation of the liver)
E026. Cholelithiasis (bile stones)
E027. fatty liver
E028. cirrhosis

### Gastrointestinal tract - Stomach and duodenal intestine
E029. Acute gastritis
E030. Chronic gastritis
E031. Stomach bleeding
E032. Ulcus ventriculi and duodenal ulcer
E033. Condition after gastric surgery

### Gastrointestinal tract - oral cavity and esophagus
E034. Stomatitis
E035. Esophageal carcinoma (esophageal cancer)
E036. Refluosophagitis (heartburn)

### Special diseases
E037. Phenylketonuria (PKU)
E038. Rheumatic joint diseases

### Metabolism
E039. Obesity (overweight)
E040. Diabetes mellitus
E041. Eating disorders (underweight)

### Fat metabolism
E042. Hypercholesterolaemia (increased cholesterol level)
E043. Hepatic Encephalopathy

### Heart and circulation
E044. Arteriosclerosis (arterial calcification)
E045. Heart insufficiency
E046. Hypertension
E047. Hyperuricaemia and gout

### Changed nutrient requirements
E048. In case of fever
E049. For malignant diseases
E050. After burns
E051. Radiation and chemotherapy

# CANCER
E052. Pancreatic cancer
E053. Bladder cancer
E054. Blood cancer (leukemia)
E055. Breast cancer
E056. Colorectal cancer
E057. Gastric cancer
E058. Kidney cancer
E059. Esophageal cancer

# TCM
E060. Bladder - moisture heat in the bladder
E061. Bladder - moisture and cold in the bladder
E062. Bladder - emptiness and cold in the bladder
E063. Large intestine - external cold affects the large intestine
E064. Large intestine - moisture heat in the large intestine
E065. Large intestine - heat blocks the intestine II acute
E066. Large intestine - dryness of the colon
E067. Large intestine - Yang deficiency (cold)
E068. Heart - Blood insufficiency
E069. Heart - Blood stagnation
E070. Heart - Fire
E071. Heart - Hot mucus clogs the heart pores

E072. Heart - Cold mucus clogs the heart pores
E073. Heart - Qi deficiency
E074. Heart - Yang deficiency
E075. Heart - Yin deficiency
E076. Liver - Ascending Liver Yang
E077. Liver - Blood deficiency
E078. Liver - Blood stagnation
E079. Liver - Moisture heat in liver and gall bladder
E080. Liver - Fire
E081. Liver - Gall bladder Qi-Empty
E082. Liver - Cold in the liver meridian
E083. Liver - Qi stagnation
E084. Liver - Wind
E085. Liver - Wind with ascending liver Yang
E086. Liver - Wind with blood anemic
E087. Liver - Wind with extreme heat
E088. Lung - Qi deficiency
E089. Lung - Mucus-moisture in the lungs
E090. Lung - Mucus-heat in the lungs
E091. Lung - Mucus-cold in the lungs
E092. Lung - Dryness of the lungs
E093. Lung - Wind-heat attacks the lungs
E094. Lung - Wind-cold affects the lungs
E095. Lung - Yin deficiency
E096. Stomach - Bloodstagnation
E097. Stomach - Fire
E098. Stomach - Cold with liquid
E099. Stomach - Nutrition stagnation
E100. Stomach - Qi deficiency
E101. Stomach - Rebellious Qi
E102. Stomach - Yin Emptiness
E103. Spleen - Heat and moisture attack the spleen
E104. Spleen - Coldness and moisture affects the spleen
E105. Spleen - Qi deficiency
E106. Spleen - Qi deficiency + Declining spleen Qi
E107. Spleen - Qi deficiency + spleen does not control the blood
E108. Spleen - Yang deficiency
E109. Kidney - Heart and kidney no longer communicate
E110. Kidney - Jing deficiency
E111. Kidney - Kidneys cannot receive the Qi
E112. Kidney - Qi is not stable
E113. Kidney - Yang deficiency
E114. Kidney - Yin deficiency


For further information visit di-book.com.